*Colophon
of the Rover*

OTHER BOOKS by Charles Edward Eaton

POETRY

The Bright Plain
The Shadow of the Swimmer
The Greenhouse in the Garden
Countermoves
On the Edge of the Knife
The Man in the Green Chair

SHORT STORIES

Write Me from Rio
The Girl from Ipanema
The Case of the Missing Photographs

CRITICAL BIOGRAPHY

Karl Knaths: Five Decades of Painting

Colophon
of The Rover

Poems *by* **Charles Edward Eaton**

South Brunswick and New York: A. S. Barnes and Company
London: Thomas Yoseloff Ltd

© 1980 by A. S. Barnes and Co., Inc.

A. S. Barnes and Co., Inc.
Cranbury, New Jersey 08512

Thomas Yoseloff Ltd
Magdalen House
136-148 Tooley Street
London SE1, 2TT, England

Library of Congress Cataloging in Publication Data

Eaton, Charles Edward
  Colophon of the rover.

  I. Title.
PS3509.A818C58   811'.5'4   78-75303
ISBN 0-498-02324-9

Printed in the United States of America

To Isabel

CONTENTS

ACKNOWLEDGMENTS

I wish to thank the following for having given me
permission to quote from copyrighted material:

Beloit Poetry Journal for permission to reprint "Banana
  Republic" and "The Amazon."
Bennington Review: "The Blue Man."
Boston University Journal: "Spanish Melon."
The Centennial Review: "The Manicurist."
College English: "The Cauliflower" and "Five O'Clock
  Shadow."
Confrontation: "The Exhibitionist."
The Georgia Review: "Biography of a Still Life," "Notes for
  an Illustrated Life," and "Squatter's Rights to the Marine
  Lands."
The Hollins Critic: "Pomegranate," "Birth of the Ox,"
  "The Dagger Thrower's Assistant," "The Hairdresser,"
  "Overleaf for Illustration," and "Collected Works of an
  Erotic Author."
The Kenyon Review: "The Ox in Autumn" and "Life Cycle
  of a Top Hat."
The Malahat Review (Canada): "Incident in the Garden"
  and "The Man in the Decadent Picture."
Michigan Quarterly Review: "The Muscle Builder."
Poetry Northwest: "Tree Surgeon" and "Water Therapy."
Salmagundi: "The Chandelier" and "The Finger Bowl."
The Sewanee Review: "At the Mercy of Myth" and "Inland
  without Letters in Autumn."

Shenandoah: " 'The Swimming Hole' " and "Blue Bedspread."

Southern Humanities Review: "The Canoe," "The Good Wife," and "The Cuckold."

The Southern Review: "Anatomy of an Explosion" and "The Choker."

Southern Poetry Review: "Life Among the Natives," "The Pigmy," and "Medusa."

Southwest Review: "The Giraffe" and "Peacock Chair."

Texas Quarterly: "Loose Mountain Lake."

Acknowledgments are also due to the following magazines for permission to reprint one or more poems: *American Weave, Blue Unicorn, Dalhousie Review* (Canada), *Discourse, Four Quarters, Icarus, The Little Magazine, Midwest Quarterly, Pebble, Poem, Poetry Now, Quartet, Red Cedar Review, Saint Andrews Review,* and *The Voyeur.*

Also, "The Giraffe" was reprinted in the Fiftieth Anniversary Issue of *Southwest Review* and included in the *Best Poems of 1975 Anthology* (Pacific Books). Also included are parts of a long poem entitled "Five Études for the Artist" from the November 1972 issue of *Art International.*

"Collected Works of an Erotic Author", published in *The Hollins Critic,* and "Seascape with Book Ends," published in *The Arizona Quarterly,* were included in the *Anthology of Magazine Verse and Yearbook of American Poetry,* 1980, (Monitor Book Company).

"Colophon of the Rover," published in *The Arizona Quarterly,* won the Annual Award for the best poem published in the 1977 issue of the *Quarterly.*

Colophon
of the Rover

1   *A Land of Sea and Fruit*

Banana Republic

The man looks like a hood from Chicago,
Dark, thick, saturated in his own oils.
Though they abound, he eats a banana
Like the only one, with absorbed interest.
Oblivious of heat, the dusty road,
Aware the natives eat iguana meat,
He likes the palm's sound of green knives clashing,
The sea colored like droppings from the sky.
This is the sort of climate he admires
Where men eat bananas undisturbed
Among iguana hunters, embezzlers.
He likes to be pointed at by tourists,
Somewhat lecherous to share his life—
It would be absurd to offer them regrets.
He eats his banana slowly, peeling
Back the skin, holding it like a yellow
Lily with a speckled beige eye that grows
Till it is slack and wilted in his hand.
But the tourists know he is up to something—
Suppose he sees a creamy, lissom nude
Rising from the peeled-back skin—in this dry land
A Lady of the Lake, hiding her breasts—
There in the sun a ripe meeting of minds.
They know why he came to this republic:
To eat a banana on a hot porch
And make them think it holds a naked girl.

Once they are sure he has this kind of loot,
The world's newspapers will not let him alone,
The government will do its best to extradite—
Let there be speckled lilies everywhere,
Wholesale traffic in Ladies of the Lake—
The man contents himself to be on view.
There are no émigrés, missing persons,
A naked girl rises from every hand.
Nevertheless it was better to eat
The fruit than leave it to rot like a corpse
On the table, redolent of some grief.
So he must share the girl they think he sees,
Eat iguana with the natives just to find
If there is anything more potent than his dream.

Pomegranate

—It purges envy and hatred, Mohammed said:
Eat the pomegranate—I had a desert in my mouth
That day when the compact fruit offered me its head.

I needed a passion, oh, how I needed one that did not
        lacerate or strain—
I had ridden the camel much too long, stark, dry in the
        saddle:
Every jolt rammed insult upward into impacted brain.

One needs some such imagistic gesture to convey
How one feels full, too full, at the top, of bloody grain
And yet has not a single kind, courteous, loving thing to
        say.

There is that fruit, gracious granada, this outward thing
        that inwardly refreshes, cools,
But only as sipped syrup does beneath the shaggy tree

While babbling fountains in the sun come from the mouths
   of fools.

It is all there—the unpomaced flesh, the incomparable
   seed—
I would give two halves of a brain if I could calmly split it
   with you
That you might see the legend of containment bleed.

I do not have a camel. No horse. Casus belli—a casuist of
   fruit—
I sit beside pomegranate, the host of grenadine,
   pomander's pulsing ball,
Rammed to the point of spitting seeds, a telegram in code
   when we are mute.

The Blue Man

The happy man, it seemed, was turning blue,
Sitting in a white chair among books, bibelots.
Had he been drinking too much wine, the juice
Working its way to the surface like mercury?
Had he kissed the purple dahlias once too often?
Even a Kleenex turned blue in his hand,
The swollen veins mapping out a Land of Dusk.
The old lyric song is a choked bubble:
You have seen men spitting their purplish blood
In a basin—the hemorrhage of happiness.
Nevertheless, they insist upon more wine,
A dark blue statue somewhere in us all,
Incredible grotesque, silted, hung with grapes.
You can see it there at the end of the day
At the moment when you pour the first drink,
Send up the blue flag from a cigarette.
Ah, lovers of white chairs, books, bibelots,

Secret students of sedimentation,
The tongue has measured where the delta spreads,
The blood has learned to feed that great, far stone.
We are turning back now each bright morning,
Holding up clusters of grapes in the sunshine,
Coming home with a briefcase of smeared paperwork.
Study yourself in that chair lifting the inkwell,
Ready to flood the aquarium like a squid—
This is a magical pursuit if you
Do not falter—I knew a blue man once,
A kind of Messiah in reverse,
Who claimed that he could turn wine into water,
Though any liquid adds this color too.

Spanish Melon

The Spanish melon came, in the course of things, both
    split and chilled—
Almost impossible to describe the gelatinous arsenic-green
That seemed to advise of some sweet pleasure, being
    done with, being filled.

I search the earth for fruits that suit my mood—
Just this noontime something semisweet in death
Said: Give up the lace for cyanide—peremptory like that,
    and not a little rude.

But remember that I said the undertone was nearly sweet:
A man who lives in a cast all the way up to his neck
Can hear the smallest and the tenderest sounds that any
    fruit can bleat.

Still, why the cast, my hedonist, so heavy, without
    seam?—

The residue, the silt, from that fleet foot spreads upward,
And even melon eaters, when they feel it, know what
    calcifies the dream.

One thing is certain—you can invite the present and the
    past,
All of one's friends are artists, laissez-faire: look, let go—
Calligraphic experts all, when, you can be sure, it comes
    to writing on a cast.

But the head calls for one more slice, stays free of plaster,
Even on Salome's bloody platter having this last sweet
    thought:
I talk and talk to the thing that did me in, rather late, but
    still a master.

The Canoe

The hot trees look purplish, the river green,
The canoe, like a scimitar-shaped scar,
Seems released from the once-wounded water.
Remembering the knife, it has become
The blade, a clean surfacing noumenon—
The boy, girl, nearly nude in bathing suits,
Are the live children of a surgery,
So confident, so absolutely sure
Their making an incision, white-lipped, cool—
I can feel them cutting, cutting, tissue,
A man at large somewhat sick, stale, static,
Tense with the distance between eye and blade,
Wanting the texture pierced, turned up, yes, plowed.
The mind stands ready with its bag of seed,
But will that closing furrow germinate,
And will my presence sprout in that canoe?
The shining-limbed lovers laugh, dawdle,

[17]

Both born strong—blood donors at their ease:
Are they not, in fact, giving me their lives,
Purple trees, green river, the moving wound?
In a moment they will be out of sight;
The picture, becalmed, becomes sedative—
One must consult one's private specialist:
What visions, doctor, did your sutures sew?

The Latter-Day Crisis of Crusoe

The heavy desk held nearly everything but fate—
The large man who sat there among his portfolios of
    holdings
Had long ago decided that fatal things can wait.

His papers, legal documents, made a kind of crowded
    continent
Where ten white savages loomed, avaricious, almost
    giant-large,
Insisting that resource was virgin when others said that it
    was spent.

A single piece of paper made a brilliant map—
Could one not see how many terse directions he had
    written there
For those who only came to lie beneath the palms and take
    a nap?

What could he offer them as some inducement, yes, a
    bribe?
Here was a letter opener of gold, a silver vase of roses:
He must persuade these others that his ten would make a
    ruling tribe.

Such is the glamorous game one plays across the board—

I have seen men dreaming at their desks, steeped in tropic
    light,
Ready to give a loincloth of inkwell blue to anyone who
    would accept the minor to his major hoard.

A heavy desk, an imperious race enacted by white
    fingers—
The wind ruffles papers, a white moth chance-like rises at
    the window:
Who can be sure if fate he cannot see is setting sail or
    lingers?

The Pigmy

What a child of joy! What a brown dumpling!
There are alligators and headhunters,
But the pigmy is so deft with enclaves—
A whole foot lower in the wind, he scents
The foe before he is quite come upon.
Who from afar might not mistake his head
As vegetal, a kinky, tousled mushroom:
This is the sweet, sweet dream of being small.

Splitting melons instead of human heads,
Rinsing his smile with such fresh, florid juice,
The pigmy banishes gray connectives—
One sun, one moon, one limpid river flowing:
Such liberal pleasure from interstices!
Take a pigmy home with you and give him
Ice cream, pistachio, green as a lizard—
See how he devours a melting image.

Built up in shoes, socks, pants, belt, shirt, and hat,
The great advantages of height will count

The pigmy so many sacks of sugar,
Brown sugar mixed with cinnamon for buns.
Who wants a skin that smells too much like rum?—
The pigmy sees us eating images,
Colors of the world running from our mouths,
Like the drool of alligators, like death.

Scenario for the Sun Prince

Let him be the one that everyone suspects
Of lying on his shadow in a darkened room
And dreaming the most violent dreams, one part sunshine,
    one part sex.

Walking in the sunlit street, exuding something like a
    glare,
Accompanied by his captive shadow, he gathers all the
    power
Anyone could wish upon this insinuating pair.

He will go glistening by the windows, and the oil of eyes
Will leave on shining face and arms an extra glow, a
    sheen, a languid glamour,
And far back in a darkened house some suffocating one,
    who cannot see him, cries.

I posit thus the dreamer as one who wishes that he
    understood
How force is drawn out of the houses in the implacable
    stark light,
And each face, like a figure in the desert, is looking from a
    hood.

One hesitates and meditates a moment on the nature of the
    real—

[20]

He has gone home, all the blinds are drawn, the women
    weep in solitude:
Now all he means to answer for is what his sun-drenched
    senses feel.

The world is forgiven and forgotten like a cinematic set:
Twitch the curtains. Did he really walk his shadow home?
Knock on the door. What is the text? Are the rushes ready
    yet?

Life Among the Natives

A few white grapes, a slice of canteloupe,
The smallest cut of universal pie:
You do not need too many reasons not to die—
I drink my courage, and I eat my hope.

In straits, better settle for real life—
Put the cool grapes in the melon scoop,
Then let your morals be the willing dupe
Of rich, immaculate still life.

Juicy freedom within stricture,
One grape a hogshead of new wine:
Invite the cannibals to dine
On melons growing wild just beyond the picture.

They will not raid your orange canoe:
There is something invulnerable and just
About an honest appetite or lust—
I saw my picture, and I ate it too.

The Prime Minister's World View

The Prime Minister arrives, dark-suited,
Aware that the world is Technicolor—
One could be vatted and dyed in an instant,
Feed on sweetmeats from a mistress's moist hand,
Tent with a homosexual chieftain,
Cruise into the snake-infested heartland,
Observe the large pores of a belly dancer,
Fiddle with a tassel, be a *bonne fourchette,*
Have every close-up pounded up the nose,
And never know the rest of the fat world
Was a squashed portfolio of spoiled bonbons.
The Prime Minister is that most difficult
Of men, a highly trained, restrained taster
Of people—no greasy crumbs upon his desk.
An inkwell reminds him of an ocean,
A letter opener, the lance of a tribesman—
The Prime Minister's soul is infinitely absorbent,
Compresses full-length features into news,
Exudes a picture of the world in black and white.
There is something to be said for this view,
It gives aid and comfort to heads of state—
He can, of course, as readily see himself
With fleets of gunboats streaming from his fingers,
Tanks, submarines ramming the passive sea—
With the oil embargo lifted, relaxing,
Eating the spiced tongues of languid natives,
Sticking emeralds in buttery navels—
These fantasies racked up like billiard balls
Rebuff the curious since he holds the cue.
At the conference table he smells of civet,
A ruby in his anus to provide

When the great failed time of the criminal comes.
From his office he can watch the egos scatter:
They do not turn around the maypole now.
He can see the youths in many costumes,
Prying cobblestones to find the hidden book.
He feels like the devil when he eats their dream,
Would give them a black ribbon from his heart
If they could even string two Valentines
Together without tearing them to bits.
Let the shish kebab drip on the vest,
The wine seep like a bruise into the groin,
The world indeed, the existential wound!—
If the child laughs, knowing where the ruby lies,
There is a fat Swiss Bank account as well—
The Prime Minister wallows the daydream,
Then drains the hued gobbets from the vista—
How can he set down the brain, a crystal
Paperweight, gripped eye of the Sultan,
When he is sitting pretty, sitting warm?—
Perhaps it is nothing more than that he bilks
Toward the center, his home the centrifuge.
It would be like breathing God to see the birds
Return, the children stroke the statue's hand.

The Oasis

You do not always need to think too large, too big—
Somewhere in the world an oasis waits for you:
Somewhere your palm, your apricot, your fig.

The mind is the desert traveler par excellence.
It can go miles and miles without the equivalent of water:
The marauder that would be messiah dismounts the camel,
    puts down the lance.

It needs only a child's playpen duned with sand
To plant the phallic tree, exhort the seductive waters of
    the well,
Loosen ties with murderous rogues, and give up trafficking
    in contraband.

Above all else, it is this incredible being what we are, what
    not,
This life of saddle sores that rides a secret like a saving
    grace,
Guarding the many-folded map that takes us to our
    verdant spot.

You learned in the playpen, if you learned at all, to swallow
    secret paper in a wad.
Others destroyed the tapes, burned their documents, used
    the shredder,
And learned to go on across the sand, their body a divining
    rod.

One has thrown sand, eaten maps, paper-sick in many
    places—
Still, it is an incomparable thing this dismounting brigand
    where the secret quivers—
A cicatrice that trembles in the heart above the green
    oasis.

2 *Fabulous Relations*

The Good Wife

The good wife had married at sixteen,
Neither too late nor too soon, Husband said
On that day she entered his world forever
There among his strong, red-faced countrymen,
Her veils and bridal gown like whirling water—
The first kiss was the vortex drawing in.
So this was what it was to know a man.
His house was very strong indeed with clear,
Bright windows, one bedroom by another,
Room enough in which she could remind him
That someone not his like would live with him.
Though dreams still wore their fatal vertigo,
She cleaned and cooked and sewed like someone risen.
He took her to bed, called her a good wife:
Like a nut without a kernel, she lay
All night, filled with the fury of his love.
Quilts, rugs, jellies blazed with her emotions,
She sewed a dress a gypsy could not scorn.
But Husband stayed implacable and dark,
Glowing in the sunlight, still nocturnal.
When the good wife took out her bridal gown,
Nuzzled it, then went mooning by the pond,
That night she felt unstable in his arms
And he repulsed her as a revenant.
As she knitted by the fire, her heart beat
Like a lover in a ballad. She cried

And looked out at the haystack in the fields
As if it held the corpse of memory.
When the first child came, a son, Husband said:
The first step of a stairway we will build—
To her a pretty toy, and yet a force
To feed, another coil of manic power.
She turned him in the batter of the days,
A charming figure in a fairy cake—
That portion fell to Husband and his wish.
When the girls of the family came along,
They clung to him like motley-colored bees
Which sucked at some potent, dark, wild honey.
Nothing could free them but another man.
And it seemed to the good wife that the world,
The great stuffed world, had an iron pike in it
And was invisibly bound with iron.
Husband knew this, knew where the center lay,
Thought a man should stand there, drenching his strength
Until it throbbed against the iron hoop.
How could the good wife free him and thereby
Free herself? Her face which had been so fair
Grew brown as cider—He, though gaunt, remained
Black as the bole of a tree in autumn.
He was a good man—so it came to her
In just that way. He had not meant her harm.
He had done his best to steady the world,
Engrossed, full of nocturnal manliness.
Thus, her girlhood dreams ventured back in time
And she could see them both, free, transparent,
The stuffing of the world, fruits and flowers,
Through them and beyond them—Elysian fields
Where the long burdened mating was over
And the dark amatory harmony
Was dissolved, the great purpose of the earth
Would grant the good wife one last wish to see
Her lover as she would somehow have him be,

Not centering the world but at the rim
With her, sharing the vista that she had
When love was far, far from the heart of things.

House at Twilight

Today, Bluebeard fools no one with his lavish oriental
    dress
And authoritarian virility. That gesture of giving the key to
    his latest wife
Looks like nothing so much as a compulsion to confess.

Even our villains, so it seems, have gone to seed.
Curiosity not only killed the cat—it opened
Our legends far too wide and made them bleed.

Rather than hear our women calling tenderly, Bluebeard,
    come back, come back,
As if the locked room were crucial to happiness,
We sit in a perfectly open house, the resident, unrepressed,
    hemophiliac.

He was, after all, just a man who had a problem with a
    blue-black beard,
Essentially a lurid, extreme manifestation of five o'clock
    shadow,
And yet, more than anything on earth, he wished to be
    revered.

Does this suggest that when we had much more to hide,
Lush, beheaded corpses dumped like silk sacks in a room,
We maintained a tension that did not lead us blandly to
    deride?

Strange, though, when the house is flooded with sun and
    the heart feels light and drained
How blue the evening nudges some stray feeling a woman
    has aroused,
And one could swear she hides the key in hand, indelibly
    blood-stained.

The Amazon

This is a myth utterly conceived by males—
One day the grown boy will meet the Amazon,
A handsome girl enlarging before him,
The whole world suddenly getting out of hand,
The secret pituitary code mastered,
The entire adaptive situation altered.
Who will curl in under his powerful arms,
Whose eyes will meet the eyes upon his chest?
The boy considers desperate measures:
The girl should wear a capstone on her head,
Giving some great, harsh ceiling to her sex,
A caryatid set upon a porch
Where men discuss the matters of the world.
But the girl keeps growing and disrobing,
Threat, seduction, in an hyperactive loom—
Could God, the Man himself, now stunt her growth?
The boy cannot accept supportive role,
His ego delicate as the sperm he bears.
The woman who wears the tight, applied myth
Undresses forever and still must grow—
The girl studied the arts of reduction,
But the woman pushed her head against the sky.
It was only when remembering boyhood
The man could ever put a stop to it,
The time before the ground was strewn with fetishes—
An early morning glow just to seeing,

No thought of what would be, preponderate—
The girl stroked him, a tassel in the wind,
No sacked cities yet, ruins to contemplate—
The girl washed her stockings in the river,
The boy dropped the stone carried in his hand,
His body like a lovely, lidless eye.

Ironies of an Aging Dwarf

Wasn't it enough for a lifetime to have been small,
Overbranched and overshadowed by all my friends
Who now boom in their illness and, like dead or dying
    trees, threaten to fall?

They had all the high, open, free spaces, I, the moss.
I was even half in love with their swaying, rustling
    whisper,
And never prepared myself to be the recipient of such
    great rain of loss.

Protected from the sun, I could see the moon through the
    leaves
Looking for something small, yet unobserved, to love,
And I could imagine it was only the large who largely
    grieves.

They took and took, I told myself, from every tiny
    giver—
I did not stint them the flow of my figurine heart
Until they felt me in their roots as trees do the infatuate,
    swollen river.

But now, together, we have run our course—
Old as well as small, an exhausted pod upon the ground,
I must spend my hours reviewing the dark philosophies of
    force.

Did I, in the overview, lack the brute resources to be tall,
Or was I better off, tolerated, nourished, and caressed,
By those who did not love among themselves, not ever
    having to account to anyone at all?

The Cuckold

Why shouldn't the other fellow wear the horns?—
He is the satanist, the liar, the cheat.
Like Mephistopheles, he comes in dreams
And I wake up shaking in my bed,
Wondering if Sleeping Beauty has been gored,
Feeling my head to see if it is smeared
With blood. Her nightgown is not smudged or torn;
She lies with her soft hand below her throat
As if to strangle any telltale sighs.
Her garter belt dangles across the chair,
Obscene as a straightjacket. I search
For unrolled condoms tossed beneath the bed—
I cannot remember, I mix three lives—
Once in the street, I prowl a loose world
Of fatuous transference. The delivery boy,
The postman, the man in his business suit,
Are animals turned upon their tamer.
I knew them all, once—slinking and passive,
As the day turned round me like a cage—
How is a man to rightly wield a whip?—
Nothing is inclosed, the mind runs with its own animals.
At home, she works, sings, holds her jellies
Up into the light as though they were jewels
Of her simplest nature, a pictured scene
That one might pierce with voodoo pins and find
They stuck the heart upon a stranger's chest—
Titterings and whisperings where no sound is,
The turning of a key behind a door,

Clapping some startled lounger on the back,
Sleeping in lime beside a muffled form—
"She is sister to Lazarus. She must
Come back into a life free of the sores
I wear upon my face like eyes"—She sighs
As though the man who floats above her hears.
I lie like a pajama suit cast off
And hope that she does not know that I am there.
She might forget, God knows she might forget,
And take me for the one whose head wears only curls.

At the Mercy of Myth

Do not refuse to know the many ways of love—
Leda trodden by the swan did not shun such knowledge;
Peace may be begotten in copulation with the dove.

Now so much is given to review, rehearse,
That History may come to seem monotonous
And cloak our eyes to anything unique as though it were
    perverse.

This is not to say strange lovers are required—
Happy are those who find the simple down of humankind
Mythical enough and far more to be desired.

But there are those who search the ordinary skies
For someone brilliant as a Mercury on wing,
An incognito form of rapture colored like a bird of
    paradise.

Decorum in its grace can lead us into error,
With all of its rightness make us choose the worthless one
And sleep and sleep again with some revulsive terror.

So may the world's reductions keep the innocent profane:
Some few who do not fear the wingbeat at the window
Will look for the golden feather where their lover's head
    has lain.

Medusa

Medusa may have been an ordinary woman,
Not particularly bright, beautiful, good.
But she had a pair of eyes, oh, indeed
She did and they brought things up short, fixed
Them, some men said—it was her eye for men
That made her notorious in the countryside.
They somehow did not feel like men anymore,
Stripped down, naked, like castrated statues,
But still too soft and lifelike for her taste.
Passing by, she stamped on a broken hand
As if it might wriggle off, slink away;
One man became the future with a sigh
And made his peace within an attitude—
That, she remarked, was progress of a sort.
Little by little the world itself seemed stolid,
Sculpturing itself beneath her eye and yet ruined.
The branch of a tree and an athlete's arm
Were equally heavy, action merely implied,
Something that had been. The sweat in the armpit,
The pollen, had dropped but would drop no more.
Thickening, hardening, strangely the world was much,
Much smaller, time viscous, and Medusa
Grew her first head of snaky hair—anything
To repel and yet attract whatever moved.
She began to have difficult breathing
For her own members had been affected,
Draped in stone except for her mobile eyes.
This was all a long time ago. The world

Kept breaking out of mold and one fierce spring
She thought the hemorrhaging would never stop.
Many Medusas later, Perseus appeared,
Wandering into the stone world like a boy
Who feared but loved the past. She gasped, groaned,
She could not stand this shining seed pod
On the marble floor. The snakes did a war dance
On her head. She felt fitfully alive.
But Perseus looked backward through his shield,
And one would give much to see the amalgam
That he saw, face upon face, a congeries of eyes,
The throes of a thrashing stony world,
Limbs bleeding at the same time that they petrified.
Just before he struck, he saw the view beyond the shield,
The green world without stricture flowing.
This, too, was many Perseuses later,
And to this day there are those who feel one foot
Heavy, one foot fleet, the landscape burdened
Or buoyant, giddy with the wildest dreams.
Medusa, the greatest spendthrift ever known,
Has left us nothing but a pair of eyes.

The Rhododendron Story

When the man had gotten over his romantic phase,
Or thought he had, someone asked him about his
        rhododendrons.
It was known all over town he had been their amorist.

They humped on his lawn like the pink mosques of a
        religious fanatic.
Many reduced it to the level of collecting stamps or milk
        glass,
But others, only a few, thought they might have a muezzin
        on their hands.

[33]

They rather liked to suppose they could hear an exotic call
     to worship—
Though they did not know it, the man selected these few
     for his soul's city:
A mania is always born in the hearts of a few adherents.

As there are varieties of religious experience, so with
     rhododendrons.
He made the call from the tower, but they did not need
To come in flowing white robes and knock their heads on
     the ground.

Meanwhile, the collectors of milk glass had a point—
They wanted to know in what important way obsessionals
     differ.
Pink stamps in an album look better than pressed
     rhododendron petals.

So the man took an entirely unexpected tack, a new lease.
He bought an album, put some hideous knobby objects in
     the window,
And everyone in town immediately lost interest in him.

Thus religion, or what seemed to be religion, gives way to
     window dressing—
I have often told this story to myself and can in no way
     make it into a parable
Though one regrets that even a sometime, seasonal, thing
     goes by the boards.

There must be abandoned places where old men sleeping
     among newspapers,
Wild, woolly, eyes pink-rimmed and milky, remember the
     rhododendron craze,
Scratching their heads as if they knew, or thought they
     knew, a prophet in their time.

Water Therapy

Down in the doldrums with rain, rain, I went down to the
     pool
Which somehow maintained its vat of supernatural blue,
Exempt from my analysis on a day I so lusted for the
     beautiful.

It was a bath for eternal Venus. I had buried there on
     sunnier days
Thousand of thoughts, some, mere stoppages for a life
     running out—
If the times were right, I would be a man of all-desiring,
     all-absorptive ways.

What of the years one spends on definition?—I wished to
     let the load
Of water tumble through the strongest and most lucid
     form:
The bodies of women, the spiritual images, sluiced with
     monster and toad.

The charged and oblique experience that makes the
     current move!—
I do not want to slow to a halt, nor, to put it flatly, burst.
I have slept with every image that Venus herself would not
     reprove.

If the times were right—How much, in the long light of
     time, will that phrase mean?—
I strip and go brusquely toward the almost arctic blue.
If riches fall away, stick to the absolute encounter, the
     basic love scene,

As a soldier might arouse the too-scarred surface of his
     touch.

Venus has bathed here, wallowed, if you prefer, and left it
  blue, blue, blue:
The combatant in me plunges blind, throws aside the
  times as if they were a crutch.

3 Conceptions and Compulsions

Incident in the Garden

It had its thick, hot setting, all right,
The garden rabid with lush red peonies,
The fountain sounding like healthy kidneys.

One was in no sense naturally deprived,
Two very white people conversing
As though the Arctic never held its breath.

Then as if we had struck each other,
We were given a subject—Two lusty dogs
Grappled, stuck, made ineradicable love.

They were illicitly mongrelizing, of course—
Try as we would we could not pull them apart,
The male had swollen like a knob in some closed door,

Very much a part of peonies and hissing fountains.
At first we had disheveled, even murderous, thoughts.
We might have brained the thing in half again:

Something we had not willed had taken place.
It was like the Red Sea which we had held apart
Coming together in tense, mortal silence.

Getting over the shamelessness, the outrage,
We let the dogs pulse—The copula became
Secure as a plumber's fitting in our nerves.

Then it was over, a quiet door opening.
One rested in halves again, petted two
Nuzzling heads, watched two tongues drip like salmon

Hung in their mouths—We had so much wanted a subject,
And here it was, broken in two again, childlike,
Helpless, still musky with the inextricable.

The Earring Syndrome

The tall, handsome woman would hang lilacs
From her ears like bizarre, lavish pendants
If her mind could stand the opulent weight,
An elephantiasis of amethyst,
An extreme gesture that would not pull
Her to the ground—absurdly felled by earrings.
So it has been said, we walk by climbing.
The woman has built herself from ground up,
The brain could be the heaviest thing,
A purple jewel hidden in the skull.
Then why has springtime made her feel like tumbleweed,
This particular spring, vicious and mad,
When she looks the lady to everyone,
A beautifully fluted, extended creature?
So feverishly she longs for earrings,
Ah, the lush drop from either side of mind,
The exquisite, scented, natural heaviness!—

[38]

One baldly takes the psychiatric stance:
Life in our times is just not livable—
A cherished woman wanting this much more,
The incomparable bauble at the peak.
Still she moves like the proud queen of our dreams—
If we can, we see her through the mad scene,
The frightful tearing of the purple dress
As if she would pour her flesh upon the ground,
The trampling of lilacs as though they were grapes—
There was this sad, light, vacuous feeling,
The top not being what it might have been.
We give her all the earrings she desires
As if their weight would keep her where she is.

The Cauliflower

If you take it from itself, it lacks its own reclusive hull—
It rolls and rattles in the basket, postoperative and
        surgical:
You have on your unconventional hands a brain still
        looking for a skull.

This is what comes of letting mind too far and wide
        abroad,
It gets out of itself into the strangest, whitest, branching
        places,
And sees lying on the dusty ground its unprotected mother
        lode.

I do not think, at first, that this projected sight will
        please—
The man whose best-kept secret was a richly irrigated
        world
In all likelihood will not be glad to settle for a hard and
        knobby cheese.

Still, what is a man along the road to do, that inevitable
   catechumen?—
If he does not look out, let the irrigating channels flow,
The system turning on itself becomes a mist, a cauliflower
   mix, cloudy as albumen.

Certainly there must be more than our share of going in
   and out the gate:
I am a head caught in a basket or like old cheese crumbling
   in the road,
And you are fortune's favorite child, knowing when
   projected, when innate.

A thing too white and lifeless, and the living head
   withdraws—
But I have not emphatically discovered where to set the
   circle and caesura,
Or if a cauliflower, too much taken from itself, inevitably
   gives pause.

The Exhibitionist

There was so much light around always,
Always so much light. One had been brought up
To believe in candor, not to hold back
Anything, the sun an aseptic camera.
What everyone could see was limpid, clean:
The lush girl walking in her full brassiere—
Athletes committed mayhem in broad daylight,
The blue policeman swung his glistening stick.

What could one do with this uneasy sense
Of some ardent, secret oscillation,
The wavering echo of lucid shapes?
Only a few could see the dark angel

Wandering through the world, striking at glass chimes.
The exhibitionist wearing an eye shade
Kept watch along the street and the bright field,
Listened for the sigh that bubbled out of glass.

Finally a girl came by and wavered
Much as if the blue man struck her with his stick.
The exhibitionist felt music fly
From his mind like a dizzy swarm of bees—
You and I sit in a sunny, toneless room
And tell his story: The girl was one of us.
She came crashing back from the shrill, dark wood,
The man fell pommeled by the burdened tree.

The Deaf-Mute

We, too, are revoked by the way he understands—
Banked up orally, our ears plugged with the hardened,
    resinous gum of sound,
We jerk inwardly with repressed desire to be talking with
    our hands.

We want to place our fingers on another's moving lips,
Tap on our palms, make strange, gnostic notations:
We must find the devious route for our profoundest
    thought, the paltriest of our quips.

Yes, for a moment, but, oh, what a difference when we
    turn, at bay,
Inundate the jeweled lady with our lavish compliments,
Let the words flow like semen and with her have our
    way—

Until at midnight or some such final and exhausted hour,
Hearing the lovely lady still talking like an enchanted doll,

You have strange castrative doubts about your virile
    power.

You listen then only to her beautiful gesticulating fingers
And wish that she would feel some secret, stifled vibrato
    on your lips
As if something that you wished to say still palpitates and
    lingers.

You go to the window to look at the stars, and see one
    shoot—
It is as if you had released it yourself without a word or
    any sound at all
And the lady by your side were loved beyond all
    reckoning, and deaf, and mute.

The Chandelier

It looks rather like a crystal fruit tree
With all of those clear pear drops hanging down,
An upside down tree, of course, a reverse,
The long stem stuck in a soil of plaster.
There is good reason to think it may fall,
A sense of excessive weight, a kind of angst—
Perhaps a good death, buried in diamonds,
But, just perhaps, a lifetime of waiting.

But if one tries to further humanize,
The image is androgynous. This could
Be a skirt of rhinestones spirited aloft
By the most implacable of voyeurs.
The house shakes with someone heavy walking:
The chandelier, vaguely testicular,
Would wince if you struck the dangling lustres,
And make a kind of tinkling, cruel music.

The rich sun, of course, wants a peacock,
The breeze ruffles the prismatic tail:
So many hands at the bag of brilliance—
As for me, I prefer the long waiting,
The wondering when the fireworks really start,
The dazzling tension building forever,
Less tree than loaded, suspended fountain—
I am in love with images that loom.

The Pink Cloth

The woman thought: No, I will not, today I cannot, and
    then she could:
The setting up, the simple logistics, a pink cloth laid across
    the table,
In the center, like eyes watching every move, a bowl of
    dogwood.

The trick, she had learned, was to feel the color first,
    before the mind could think.
Another time it would be iris with green, or blue and
    yellow;
Now it could be nothing else but judgment day of white on
    pink.

Nevertheless, she had to put it to herself as would an
    engineer—
After the pink *banderilla* stuck the brutal, indolent, sensual
    life,
Panache would have to see her through as if, in this
    respect, she had no peer.

Sometimes the simplest gesture, then, requires the service
    of a matador:
No, I will not, today I cannot, and then, I must,

The eyes of dogwood watching her in lieu of that strained
    place where thousands roar.

We come into the room, without pique, and sit down at the
    table,
Drink a glass of wine the color of a thick bull's blood,
Obtuse, or just a genial passing glance upon the surface of
    a fable.

Bless this woman in her weary, wary, always watchful,
    wit—
The pink cloth, the dogwood—the pittance given for the
    daily keep:
You do not know it, but her white hand open on the table
    is where the Furies sit.

Tree Surgeon

He is the man who trims our overworld—
Through windows we desire a bloated life,
The fullness of time, women, color, love.
The man in the knickers, boots, operates;
A huge arms falls, a leafy hand, a foot.
The great *docteur sauvage,* the criminal
Has never admitted to malpractice.
Without any fear of complications
He eats his lunch among the flesh and bones
And drinks a beer, smokes a cigarette,
In his own kind of carnage quite at ease—
Of course at home he is another man,
Tangled in the arms of his soft, plump wife,
Mired in the thicket of those brash children.
There is a window, too, that thickly bleeds.
He remembers the houses where he worked,
The style, insouciance, the *joie de vivre.*

A surgeon to the very careless rich,
He illustrates philosophy for them,
Tailors the common heritage of trees.
Taking the saw from the pale suicide,
He cuts just so much away, nothing more.
We recuperate, we regain the trees,
Toned, tightened, painted with black beauty spots.
It is a theater of operations—
He keeps our trees reasonably healthy, whole.
We cannot tell him not to slap his wife,
Reproach him with his fat and dirty children:
Constant, perfect, he never claimed to be.

Birth of the Ox

Some people think that patience passes over into being
    dumb,
But the greatest passions know this is not so—they push
    through the real,
Solidly forming as they go, horizontally accreting,
    plunging plumb.

From the time the bull left his thunderous cloud in her the
    ox knew this well—
The powerful gesture feeds on the mystery of matter,
Possibly considers what forms it might take if the code in
    the tornado of sperm won't jell.

Beneath all others, then, this overture to mind
To take upon itself entrails, pelt, the absolutely curious
    shape:
Everything packed in, not too much, too little—nothing is
    left behind.

Nevertheless, when the ox drops her baby, she licks him
    clean.

One might say a certain culture begins right then, right
    there;
If it were not so necessary and natural, it would be
    obscene—

She grooms a being pushed from a place of excrement.
But we are too in love with the embedded mystery not to
    make
The fantastic inductive leap from gross to heaven-sent.

This is the final cushion for our wounds and shocks—
There is sweet air, an incredible spaciousness outside the
    place
Where, in our ever-fecundating, parturient guise, we
    clean the smears of process from the ox.

The Blind Man

His eyes are restless as unhatched eggs—
He wants twigs, air, and the warm soft bosom
Of a bird of paradise upon his face
Or some small, much less flamboyant creature
With delusions of grandeur. Around this wish
Things are much too dark, creative, sexual,
A sense of ducts and membranes everywhere.
Music is a skinful of vibrations—
Everything bursts from its shell beyond him:
He can only think of his face as a nest.
Once he has not heard from the aviary,
The day is a festering zoo of action,
Everything having been born, delivered,
The voices like grunts and snarls beside him—
So can the man who sees believe it is:
Someone contains the stuffy, unseen world,
And we shall continue to grasp our life

In fragments, lonely, disparate, asexual.
The blind man cranes his neck up like a tree,
Our shadow blots the incubating sun—
What, indeed, would we do without the *other?*
There are, perhaps, the beautiful elect
Who lie all night beneath the gorgeous bird
To rise and walk into the crowded garden
With lyric creatures singing in their face.

The Giraffe

Not one more animal, someone said, not one more—
And I agreed, having put a padlock on my private zoo,
When there was the delicate, left-out giraffe peering
     through the door.

I had to give in, I had to yield, I had to laugh—
One cannot leave out anything, one simply cannot:
If you do, you'll find the shingles of your house, in lieu of
     leaves, attracting the giraffe.

This demoiselle with a neck so long it sways
Lets her hobbled body crumple forward as it moves,
Too thin at the same time that her style is cramped by
     stays.

Go up to the second story, look the elongated darling in
     the face,
Tell her life is short and art is very, very long,
And, lacking elevator shoes to love her, you have, alas,
     not acted altogether in good grace.

It is good for art and even better for the soul
To climb up where the left-out have to look
And wear forever their tender, alienated faces on a pole.

No doubt the door cannot always be kept open, just in
    hope, just by chance,
Yet nothing but good can come of a quick, redemptive trip
    upstairs
For the high and lonely view of those who must conduct
    on stilts their version of romance.

4 Some Worldly Ones

The Dagger Thrower's Assistant

Have you ever been the human target for another,
Stood even for a moment at the end of a perspective
Where a knife comes toward you like a traveling
    metaphor?

Here the only mercy is to be beside the point—
The dagger thrower is a powerful man with precise nerves:
No tottering, no apocalyptic sounds from creaking joint.

He wears an open flowing shirt, fresh shaven and dashed
    with lotion,
A sex symbol more than confident of his mark—
As long as I look smart, I can dress in anything except
    emotion.

I do not know just what persuades me to present
My body to a ruthless hail of steel
Except that he persuades me what he wants in my intent.

But here am I, without a shadow, still a stranger,
No edges blurred, no tufts, ripped seams—outlined in
    knives—
A post strung with invisible wires that have no other
    message but pure danger.

Still, when the handsome dagger thrower takes me on his
    arm,
Leaving my impression on the board, I feel somehow less
    gross,
More lithe, more lovable, more true to undeflected sense
    of form.

The Manicurist

Giving these hands their paid, clandestine life,
The manicurist works an illicit place,
A kind of speakeasy for manual lust—
Have you heard her talking with her clients,
Sotto voce as if police may raid
The shop and find her making book with flesh?
They hover over the bowl—her tools small
But lethal-looking for the getaway.

It is amorous too—sleek, briskly deft
Mini-massages for ten complacent nudes.
Where else can one be played with in public,
Voyeur, exhibitionist, rolled in one?
If a finger wants peace and privacy,
It can go looking for a stuffy glove—
This is a covert place with a light on it:
After the striptease, a trade in diamonds.

Sometimes the manicurist has her doubts,
Too much the psychiatrist's, confessor's fence.

Her clipped voice goes dulcet, dovish, pink-toned:
She is snipping petals from aging flowers,
Rings returned like crowns to rightful owners—
One can learn too much about the life of hands:
Money across the table is folded,
A note a lover leaves beside the bed.

Peacock Chair

He is a robust man of middle years and thick black hair:
A builder of dams perhaps, a banker, a well-known athlete
    past his prime—
One would not expect to find him, with such aptitude,
    sitting in the peacock chair.

But there comes a time of amassed life that has its sense of
    dearth.
One has been around the track once too often in such hot
    pursuit
And never once sat still, awaiting, unrelieved, the message
    from the ends of the earth.

Yet everything is starkly now, so much a present tense—
At the risk of seeming mannered, one would sit in a chair
    with a spreading fan,
The glossy head dreaming of some drenched halo—a
    laddered iridescence.

The dun-colored rattan chair is only an abstract basket
    weave,
But here in a place beyond words, or where words have
    never arrived,
The man who is full of the world has chosen the moment
    to grieve.

In an incredible act of mimesis, without uttering a word,
Every hair on his body tingling omniscience, he lets out
    the suppressed rainbow,
And we see the man of affairs becoming the glistening
    bird.

Perhaps for just this reason we have spared such props as
    these—
The absurdly beautiful peacock chair, the man,
    self-stuffed, self-stopped, suddenly hallucinating,
And the powerful, beseeching messenger from the ends of
    the earth, come begging on his knees.

The Stickpin

If nothing else, it gave him the effect
Of a little third eye on his hard chest.
Moonstone, faded opal, bleached amethyst,
It was not meant to be too color-fast.
One gets the true shade of the natural eye,
Shifts quickly to the small ambiguity.
If one found a diamond there it would seem
Too much the flashy button of his brain.

The man with the casual stickpin says,
Here is a little groin of sensation,
Not a soft thing, an easy thing, after all,
But a sort of third eye for a third world,
A pin set down upon a secret map.
Preferably it goes with clipped moustaches,
A scar on the cheek and erect bearing—
Not just any man should wear a stickpin.

Perhaps only one in a large gathering,
Loose, luscious as a full-blown peony,

And perhaps he should merely brush the mind
With a foppish, military image.
Someone will let him out at the back door
And carry the lizard look of the pin
Into the great put-together flower
Which wanted so deeply this tough voyeur.

Five O'Clock Shadow

Such a fat, glorious world and there the lean, unpublished
    manuscript—
I saw the poet sitting on his porch opulent with flowers
    and fruit:
Why does he look ink-stained in blue shadow when he is
    so handsomely equipped?

This is the inherent, hapless ambiguity of scene—
He has written the poem and still is sponsored by the
    flower;
His hand loaded with words is reaching for the fostering
    nectarine.

You know the absolute engagement with a luscious fruit,
The pansexual power in the touch and scent of flowers:
The body vocalizes, vocalizes, vocalizes, and still the
    book is mute.

His is a very special case perhaps, and yet not quite—
I have seen our other potent counselors sitting in their
    private arabesques
With a rich, avaricious, and deluded sense that they have
    not yet got it right.

There in the blue light the white hand in a stain—
Our bulging satchels and our thin, aborted manuscripts

Have too much in common not to be a meeting of the
    twain.

Could it be a rather ordinary fate, this disillusion with the
    Book of Hours?—
I doubt it, since the two make more than special
    claims—ink-stained and anxious—
Neither one the fatal and resigned purveyor of dried fruit,
    pressed flowers.

The Muscle Builder

At first, it was largely horticulture—
One is so poorly seeded and tubered
To begin with—packets of misadventure.
So you need a mirror for this garden;
It must be watched at one glossy remove.
It is a perverse plot, too fat, too thin:
The muscle is a glorious nematode,
Humping secretly, without head or tail.

Underground, bronze dahlias thump toward the sun,
The neck strains watering the mental system:
One sets out dried blood to scare the animals.
At last the muscle builder is in bloom,
Carrying himself like a full flower stall.
At this ripe point, his compleat science ends.
Either you buy or you don't. There may
Be a very short season in muscles.

So if he lives, he must diversify,
Rippling his arms like the necks of gold swans.
But ornithology will not quite do.
Is there a harp hidden in his sinews?
The vital innards seem to pluck themselves—

This stunted student is our favorite child.
We dress him, undress him, put him to bed,
Humoring his pleas for crop rotation.

The Oldest Lover in the World

The man, so he thought, was finished, through with
        touch—
Someone had drawn the liquid from the battery,
Someone had cut the hyacinth hanging in his crotch.

A nude was rather like a stilted bathroom fixture:
One could turn the faucet-breasts, wait for the sound of
        water,
Sunk, subterranean somewhere, stolid underneath a
        white-tiled picture.

Walk, don't run. Be heavy with a very old desire,
Have a magic lantern in each eye projecting dashing
        figures,
Taking off their clothes as they reach the square where
        limbs of lovers make a leaping fire.

Better still, stand in place, let the rich and maculate day
Pull out the pockets, ruffle hair, tug at ties and laces
As if it did not mean this rigid anchor of a man to stay.

The dead cells, the pink hyacinth, the water subjected by
        harsh tile—
What is a man to do in this grave and gravid hour
But stand in line again as though he meant to run that
        extraordinary mile.

You may have seen him wiping lanterns like the lens of
        eyes,

Turning the exotic handles in that final and perfervid
    bathroom
As if in spite of all, and *au contraire,* he knows just where
    the hidden river lies.

The Hairdresser

To luxuriate and yet shape and shear—
The hairdresser, the most tactile of men,
Would give you the loose world for a fetish.
He has caressed his way into a corner,
Bathes his quick hands in disheveled fountains,
Lets them slide like bathers down golden falls.
This revelry, this reverie, comes first,
This drenching everything one is in hair.

He is the man whose hands are never sated.
He can use the shears, yet not cut off his source,
The measured stream as long as life itself—
Some say longer, as though death revered his touch.
It can be argued that he plays with life
And does not dip his fingers deep enough.
If there is something to be said for this,
Phrenology would founder on a hairless skull.

Perhaps you are nothing but a brilliant head
To him, but at least you are this, a font—
Someone dreams you in a bright pool of hair,
An unformed lady of the lake, dredged up:
Still wet, yielding, you are worked in gesso—
Life indeed is lived in such odd corners,
Obsessive stuff retrieved from the Medusa,
At the mercy, the knack, of artful hands.

Blue Clown

He is the only one among his brothers who wears blue—
His tights are smooth and lustrous as the skin of a tulip;
The eyes, shimmering with violet, look out of the blue
    makeup, rooted in that color too.

You and I wear colors of any shade or kind:
Whatever adornment, camouflage, we use is never
    constant,
But the blue clown wants us to know his life is color-blind.

The powder on his face is like a blue moth's dust.
There is a glitter of false sapphire on his hat and coat;
He is an ambassador from a land whose only motto is: In
    Blue I Trust.

Why are we lured to love those who make a strict
    decision,
The rainbow dismantlers, the fanatics, the mummers of
    idée fixe,
As if, what we could never see or know, they saw with
    tunnel vision?

To carry it off, to leave an impression, impose a tone or
    taint!—
Once long ago I saw a blue clown come out into the light
And dare the soft, liquid eye to splash him with any other
    hue of body paint.

Make no mistake—the light stays blue long after the tent
    comes down—
The only question may be, for those of us who mix our
    colors as we go,
How lambent or lethal any single passion is that penetrates
    the town.

5 *Études*

Biography of a Still Life

A green bottle, a gray pipe, a very stiff and moral-looking
    tablecloth:
Somewhere in this limpid combination an abstraction
    enters—
You retreat, and say the pipe is precisely colored like a
    moth,

The bottle, a lizard's skin melted in the very hottest fire;
You take back the moral, and say the cloth is plainly
    white—
If you do not want the picture singed, why put it on the
    pyre?

So once again: the bottle is pristine, the pipe astute, the
    cloth demure.
It will not do to keep them focused, fanatically, all alone,
Though we allude, and, no doubt, rightly should, to how
    we mean to keep them pure.

Compromise: Admit into the bottle some absinthe-looking
    sort of wine,

An ember in the pipe, a stainlike shadow on the cloth—
In any manner that you move, you make a motion toward
    design.

A bottle, a pipe, and cloth, and you are powerfully
    committed:
An enormous choking, throbbing, world pushes up a sea of
    causes, claims—
To what can just these vulnerable three judiciously be
    fitted?

It is a loose, loose thing, therefore, this clarity and light,
The slightly lascivious green, cerebral gray, the rigid
    cloth—
You heard the picture talking like yourself, heard it
    clearly, and then, not quite.

The Man in the Decadent Picture

We were asked to see the man minutely—
The eyes as if they did not wish to let
In light were dull as cloudy, red-veined marbles.
The ears had thickened like sick tendrils,
The hands lay in his lap, quite comatose,
Leathery as worn gloves stuffed with scrap meat.
It was spring and the window at his back
Threatened him with a full cornucopia—
Did everything have to be experienced again?
The door stood shut just like an upright coffin.
Let spring hang all the garlands that she wished,
Wreaths, fragrant and fluffy, like lifesavers,
As long as it left him alone to sit
There like a monument, something achieved.
Of course, it might be beautiful to follow,
One vein at a time, back to the heart's source,

A naked figure bathing in the morning light,
Feeling the marble landscape thawing as you go.
And yet the horror might be the weightlessness—
One should have learned a cleverer way of coming
So that the great chunk could have been swiftly dumped,
An absolute, irrevocable marker,
While the eyes, hung like those of a china doll,
Warmed themselves upon a furious playback.
Then one adjusted the light, accustomed
The eyes to what should be their seine-like skill,
The ears to be a much more subtle filter,
As if one might have fed this figure differently
And still have kept it powerful and proud—
The man weighs in, the heaviest of athletes
Whom we know. He stands in the door to lid
His own sarcophagus, and we fly back
From him like water from a plunging stone.

Bread and Cheese

Adorned, deformed, trussed, laced, permissive, free,
The body satisfies its ineradicable, prehistoric appetites:
A voracious man and woman sit down blindly at a table,
      and they mean to see.

The great, thatched, crusty mound of bread looks lopped
      from a severed head,
A sectioned wheel of cheese is the time-bleached,
      time-softened marrow
Of some huge beast who lost his leg to give this ravenous
      pair their well-aged spread.

They want to grasp the loaf as if it were a source of light,
Eat the nearly mystical cheese to yellow-stuff the skull—
This is, without any question, the first and final right.

Much later, in another light, someone adds a glass of wine;
It is indeed like blood returning to the famished—
The eyeless ones attract a strange percipient's design.

But never, never in this world looking toward the next,
Forget the original, overwhelming ecstasy of food,
Or mistake this plundering passion for any rarefied
    pretext.

Nevertheless, it is the mystique of wine that finally makes
    the meal.
The importunate blind man swallows slowly from a lucid
    cup—
Out of the blur, companions at a table think and touch and
    feel.

The Milkmaid

One plants a certain picture in the mind—
Say it is a milkmaid among her cows,
In one hand a stool, the other a pail,
Perhaps a minatory rooster at her feet,
Set there to grow new skin on the burned mind—
Just let it breathe and move as though it lived.
Soon there will be the volley in the pail
As though her hands worked a brace of water pistols.
Her cream dress looks screened from the lustrous hide,
The whole scene smells like a baby's warm skin—
But suppose you become hopelessly addicted?
Will the fretful cocoon in the hammock
Breach the illustrational stodginess,
Recover the dreamer from the anecdote?—
One longs, lives, for the liquid moralist
Whose high ambitions for the summer flow,
For whom the milkmaid never flaws the eye

Like the cruel, static, marbling of the blind.
Surely the black humorist in the dairy
When she bears milk like Justice and her scales
Will not be quite so predictably deadpan—
The milkmaid is by no means unallied,
Knows the ceiling cherubs are lactic drunks
And the cows stand in a mess of fixative.
The dreamer, too, can be too throwaway—
The hands that grasp the teats are radical:
Their aim is deadly though they shoot with milk.

The Head at the Desk

So still, and thus so generalized, it might be his or mine.
Is it then a plaster cast which wears, improbably, a wig—
Stuck upon a pike, an armature of thought, no torso, and
    no spine?

You have no doubt seen the back of an artist's or a
    writer's head,
And thought, my God, he is nothing in the world but brain,
Wondered if he put his parts away because they suffered
    and they bled.

One asks if there were not some black closet where
He kept a teeming body like a very special suit of clothes,
Something to be called and trotted out when he would take
    the air.

Oh, how you would like to see the rictus of the mouth, the
    eyes.
How can the sensuous script go flowing down to that one
    spectral hand?—
With all the human spares at your behest you must
    anthologize.

When he writes or paints blue eyes, are his eyes just that
    shade?—
You hide in the closet with those bones and sensual fat
To see how much the suet knows about the way a world is
    made.

Dear Christ, he turns, puts down the brush or pen—
His face is bruised and smeared with tones, colors of
    selection,
And suddenly you see the suit beside you has been worn,
    not once, but often.

The Ox in Autumn

The ox I love stands in depleted gold,
The pile of leaves like droppings from his body,
Only the hangings of blood left in the oaks,
All else, the great final defecation.
You may have your own cloacal image,
But all of us can admit when the scene
Goes it goes, and somethings like the dark ox
Remains—the stark, peering head uplifted.

I do not mean to accuse the ox or us
Of eating the glorious, framed, golden world
Like vandals munching paintings in a hall,
The gold leaf flaking on neck and shoulders
As if an art destroyed struck out at us—
And yet the effect is about the same:
A set of teeth rips through the rich texture,
We the digesters with our visceral eyes.

The ox like a figure on a cigar box
Shows a fierce sense of his predicament:
He is the twice, the thrice used conduit.

I know for I have autumn in my entrails,
A long process of maculate pictures,
And so could be stamped forever standing—
I must be taken by force and imaged:
Save me the ox head at the abattoir.

Overleaf for Illustration

Now that the world is constructed, how will it be
    construed?—
I asked the one who had made it all so clear and
    unambiguous, so he thought:
Rising out of the white-leaved book the immaculate white
    nude.

It could have been a Venus who meant to cast her cool,
    amative spell—
In that stark light, the book so pearly, all but nacreous—
Up, out, she stepped almost as if the words were shell.

I had to give respect, though grudging, to my friend.
The white book, poised like a sea gull's open wings,
Could take the niggling notion on its way the moment that
    it might offend.

There in the sky, the white clamoring, the motion in rings
    and rings,
Venus who has let the shell go free—Should one be both
    ponderable and light
If, even for a moment, one would have a perfect view of
    things?

Must I always be the standing man, the one who overlooks
My friend with the lucid eye and clear, calibrating voice

Who claims a palate for this palette in the whitest of all
     books?

Was it my hand, my black hand alone, coming down upon
     his shoulder
When the page turned, Venus withered, the folded gull fell
     like a thick dark knife, and something
Rolled across the book like a pebble from an avalanche
     turning to a boulder?

"The Swimming Hole"

Eakins, too, no doubt desired the basic—
In this case, swimmers at their carefree best.
He might have said: Don't condone the morbid for itself,
     the trick
Of being morbid to have some new thing to attest.
The falling bodies could have been done inferno
Or just as falsely in a sentimental tale.
Instead he advocates the way a summer day can go
When young men sweat for things that probably will fail.
Surely he presents the saving enclave,
The dolphin-spirit in a little country town.
Can we be free and still behave?—
I wonder if the notion may not be crucially American.
And yet the picture is not forced, abruptly closed.
Mother and the sweetheart in her health nearby conceive
     the naked source.
There is some pressure in the way the moment is imposed,
But has Apollo ever shed his clothes merely in due
     course?

Sofa by Matisse

How would you like to sit in a world of dreams
With an undulant scroll of wood at your back,
Coming down to the arms, an unraveling spiral,
    languorous, seducing the seams?

Lying or sitting in a choice of plump, sleek bowers,
You have a propellent swan in a pool by your leg,
The hand like an odalisque, receptive, idly repulsing the
    flowers.

Do not say your back and bottom do not take the hint:
Thought and feeling have their locus everywhere—
Philosophy that needs largesse is always longing for the
    rare imprint.

Ah, swan, come eat a little from the unctuous hand,
The pool lapping but leaving no brackish trace of wet:
We like a picture that somewhat nudges and yet recedes at
    our command.

Still one gets a little stiff sitting in and on Matisse
Unless one has a powerful way with furniture and fabric
And takes up inner slack and slump, smoothing out a
    crease.

It might be better, hand and bottom, lying, sitting on a
    board—
Perish the thought!—and yet I once sat on a piquant
    sorrow
And came up with a color rich as any artist ever poured.

Collector's Items

How the picture ages in the sun!—
A gnarled, massive, gold-encrusted man
Unlike the impeccable swimmer whom nothing has
    undone:
A Daumier pressed from another stone;
Seen symbolically, an old, old tree of bronze
Such as the Chinese put into a landscape,
A Tree of Life whose apples fell in tons—
I would like to see him, God-preferred, taken by the nape
And set among divinity's water-figurine collections.

Or put beside a slow, revolving pool
Where the swimmer-connoisseur could come
To see how angular he looks, marked by the tool:
One man turned in such attrition, one bronze sum!
The world as water needs a very lusty hand
(As if the world as anything could do with less!).
Look at that young swimmer running loose, a dancing
    firebrand,
By war, love, or liquor crazed—choose your favorite
    stress.
Should we expect the understudy, if boldly figurative, to
    keep our old positions manned?

Notes for an Illustrated Life

Some watermelon juice, some fresh-squeezed baize—
The real protagonist of tone and tint will do
Almost anything to give a color-lining to his days.

The red and green go down together well—
The fellow is a well-known jug, a sot for green:
Men who are full and clarified produce the finest aquarelle.

[67]

Press the palm of anyone who hoards the stain—
You will sense an iridescent moisture in the hand,
Wonder if your fingertips sweat a rainbow, drip a colored
    rain.

The sun, in time, will have you stretched out dry and flat.
The green and watermelon days have run their course,
The fullest, juiciest, go lucid-still, and end up matte.

There is a respite, and you slink off like an unrepentant
    felon:
One more chance to bilk the green of green,
One more caper as you tap the sun-proof system of a
    melon.

You have your memoirs and your memory of juices—
The scene was liquid and was always going dry:
One cannot put a life in color to any other uses.

6 *Entities and Entitlements*

Blue Bedspread

A small, thin ocean for the big white man,
And yet he looks drowning in its rumpled folds—
All that we need is one large falling wave:
Through the night the insidious rhythm,
Sea monsters thrashing in our arms and legs,
The hole of the snoring mouth like a sink—
You have seen the shipwrecked at the bed's edge,
Having kicked off the ocean about dawn,
And the whole long day will seem recessive,
The world a far, blue-fringed watercolor.
Someone with a neat hand smooths the bedspread
And plumps up the white billowing pillows.
Nevertheless the man roams the swept house,
Looking for summer's seaside cottage view,
The brilliant throw of mashed blinding breakers,
The sense of the whole cloth, out there, somewhere.
No wonder we sleep so often in the throes,
The thinnest wave thick as lapis lazuli.
I have reconnoitered these vacation days,
Calling home, calling back, a swathe of blue,
Trapped it, so it seemed, on the bed at night,
The stretched-out floating, the delicious turning.
I am not to be blamed for inwardness,
The tense body thickening as the sea thins—
One starts, stirs the conceptual liquid,
Dripping the exiguous stain of exodus.

[69]

Squatter's Rights to the Marine Lands

So you have had it, have you, you and your tossing body,
   twisted lips?—
No one has yet quite strapped you down in an iron
   hospital bed,
But the convulsion rolls like a white ocean out from your
   fingertips.

So you are a hybrid, you can't make it, round or square:
Swamped, uprooted, endangered by your own excessive
   waves,
Who is there to give a damn that you, disastrously, are
   there?

The supreme irony of any one sequestered in his head
Is that the huge, implacable expansion he deploys
Sights the tidal object of return lying on a bed.

There on that white iron someone has clearly written out
   your name.
You are known across the world, it seems, for massive
   rolling moods,
And all the water you have loosed comes back to
   embrocate your fame.

White bed, pajamas, and this curious, dry, wet, skin—
I have come like a doctor feeling soggy, in galoshes,
Talked with the booming patient until he almost did me in,

And felt, like my own pulse, the trickle, the wane at
   midnight—
The white bed, two men on the sands, an ejaculated sea,
The foolish, legalistic sun that asks: Is everything all right?

[70]

The Finger Bowl

The fingers will remember everything:
How the gloves were rolled back like thick stockings
Or sleek condoms of a five-membered man,
Insatiable and hermaphroditic,
Reaching for plums, plackets, indiscriminately;
Then glad to doze, buried alive in sand,
Standing up in a sliding, dazzling dress,
A sloughing massage of tiny jewels.

Home to a table full of placid lakes,
Scattered with flowers, amorous as navels—
Dozens of nude white comrades have gathered,
The scent and smudge of journeys on their backs.
Their leap not quite like suntanned, whooping boys,
They stalk their secrets into limpid water—
One thinks of lakeside houses long ago,
How they shook with diamonds yet smelled so dank.

So much for this clear finger lake country—
Still one remembers companions in lust,
The forced baptisms, the women's long hands,
Stomachers flashing at the water line,
The napkin for loins or an altar cloth—
Our fingers live, are licked deliciously.
But the full nude scene shivers a little,
One toe testing every lake for broken glass.

Loose Mountain Lake

You are once more asked to be eloquent, astute—
Someone rolls a wrinkled melon on the white desert of the
    tablecloth,
And yellow, yellow, folded yellow, in the morning light a
    butte.

One almost any minute now expects the cattle call,
The loose jangle of spurs, stirrups, the crisp crack of a
    whip
Where the mountain rises at the pausing of an aimless
    bowling ball.

Even if you do nothing at all but merely sit,
Something will come at you out of the inevitable, implicated,
    kinetic affluence:
The world is always fielding you a sample of its wit.

Lazy cowboys of the breakfast table hunched down in
    their shoulders,
Let the blue smoke of a cigarette drift off into the arroyo,
Knowing in their bones the pebble in the boot soon will be
    attracting boulders.

Be glad, hombre, that you have the unexpected landscape
    on the table—
This is the great virile virtue of these wide open spaces:
You can pick your teeth before the mountain turns to
    rubble.

Don't sit too long though—the yellow melon seeps.
As the wet stain spreads like a lake, speak to the
    mountain:
That which is stood for, stands, and plays for keeps.

[72]

White Lace

You have seen these women like old cocottes
Wearing a frill of lace around their necks.
One stops reading the world and lets them pass;
One went from A to B to C quite clearly,
And then this woman smudged the alphabet—
That is, she brought something up out of syntax,
Right under our noses, unnameable.
Of course, one could buy it in ten-cent stores
By the yard, but not that immeasurable glissade.
One wants to shout to her: Off with your lace!
As one says to burlesque queens: Take it off!
But she is infinite and undulant;
The ruffle writhes, enlarges like a boa—
The gut reaction: Call a snake handler—
And then we let her glide and ripple pass,
Left with serviettes, doilies, antimacassars,
Things that put out the eyes of crocheters,
Hoochie koochie of the white jungle queen—
I return to my reading, plain, simple,
The slack copulation from A to Z.
Not quite the same though: There is a movement
In among the words, magnified, sinuate,
A white dazzling flexure on the still page—
Something has come up out of it to me.
I rest an elbow on an antimacassar.
What oil will my lips leave on a napkin?
On further, further, the queen steams in a pot:
I am a cannibal on leave from language.

Collected Works of an Erotic Author

The woman loved peaches, power, sun—
Wanted the dream like a lush, moist flower brushing her
    lips,
But her lover slept beside her, hard and flat as a gun.

There on the table the luscious, rouge-smeared peach,
The force of her blood, an elegance of sunlight dying in the
    room,
And this tight, hermetic man so strangely out of reach.

She spoke as in a novel: Wait for night.
Take one last look at the sun, his brown metallic skin.
Asleep in his bronze retort, he does not want my fruit and
    light.

The chapter closes, and with it all the afternoon's
    surmises—
One wonders about this—the threat of narrative—
Must we agree?—when one subsides, the power of another
    rises.

I know enough of peaches, lustrous skin and hard-as-bullets
    pit
To know she wants and dreams the literature of love,
And yet he seems to say: No bullet can be known at all
    unless you have bitten it.

Now the book is finished, between striped, dark covers,
These brilliant afternoons interleaved with musky nights:
I close my eyes and shoot as if I knew the target and the
    flesh of lovers.

Life Cycle of a Top Hat

Poets of disquiet, look to the top hat—
It is a stilled stack, an unused pipe.
Once puffing a light, invisible smoke
As if it sat on top of something live,
It is the property of magicians,
Circus impresarios, the sad clown:
You have seen the absurd, wigged, painted face,
The slanted brim precariously alpine.

Did it at last simply choke with overplus,
Gone wild with the swollen dreams of John the Baptist,
The matted head stuck in it like a damper?
We say, so much has gone up in smoke—
Rightly so—but say little of the clogged flue,
The auto-da-fé of jewels, silk stockings,
Love's lint, crimped bunting unignitable,
Crises, crux, assassinations, the smudge fire.

A mad hatter harbors the hankerer—
Your closet is stacked with these yesterdays.
Slap the flattened crown with the palm of your hand,
You have a live trade in rabbits, flowers.
Blackened chimneys belch all over town—
If you must wear a top hat, wear it nude:
It will arouse a president on his bier,
The long train, leaping fire, the tatters in the sky.

Inland Without Letters in Autumn

A letter, black and white, and no word from you since—
I grow old in the country, rake up the golden graves of
leaves,
And hoard, like a keg of hand grenades, a basket of yellow
quince.

No word from you—just white nostalgia and blackest hate.
As the leaves fall around me, I pose, an alchemist's
caricature,
These strands of hair like charcoal marks across a balding
pate.

I am so stored, settled here—Where, what you are—
another matter.
Did you take the green and cloudy blue of summer on your
back,
Flow toward the sea, violent, and as viciously as
disenchanted water?

Somcone has stopped me solid, put a golden finger in my
brain.
I take every falling leaf as a personal death, the chronic
free-fall victim—
You do not write: I watch the maples hemorrhaging again.

It is the heaviest decline—most vulnerable to shocks.
Accumulating burnished evidence against your fluent
ways,
I shall send my body to you like an ingot in a box.

Bending silver in a bar, ah, glistening fish, who never
wrote!—
I pray for an implosive sea, core it with flying fragments
As if the yellow quince could reach so far, wrapped in a
sallow note.

Anatomy of an Explosion

The room was the place a bomb exploded,
A sense of flesh flying away like birds,
The incisive pencil shot from his hand,
The alphabet splattered in foreign tongues,
His tangled clothes a fused mass of several people—
Some such extravagant thought may fuel
The mind packed with its own dismemberment.
We lie in bed all night, bronzing the past,
A corrosive green fouled by the pigeons.
You wake loaded, a little stiff with form;
How did this sore statue get in your bed?
You must melt it down even to start the day,
Until, turning, one feels the first implosion:
The tumid stomach suggests a gas mask;
Why are these muscles lead, yet high octane?
A conception of dispersal arises:
A beautiful man in tight ore—
Do not tell me you have not sometime longed
To let it go, sprayed everywhere at once,
The heavy one who wears the green pajamas.
Standing in your stocking feet, you pick them
Up again, your own discrete particulars.
It is not that you loathe the formal sense
But that lying in bed some clear morning
You have this desire to remake a man,
As if bombs go back as far as Adam,
As if birds know this flying on forever.

Seascape with Book Ends

For some strange reason, reading the yellow novel, one
    thinks of Greece—
The blue character, blue with longing for the sea,
Steps out of the pages of the book and will not give you
    any peace.

Perhaps just this touch of sunlight on the cover
Made you slip into the blue man's skin as if you had
    swallowed mercury or sea water,
And nothing in the world would make you say: All
    voyages are over.

You feel clean, swift as a fish, yet thick and dense,
Steam like a demonic statue with roseate, redolent mist,
And all extremes of power and passion suddenly make
    sense.

When was the wishful, widening wanderlust reduced to
    lust?—
Those lucid pages and the blue man mewling for the
    sea?—
When did the thing itself, like a naked root of life, rise in
    the settling dust?

One quivers, hovers, hankers for the citron land,
Brings it all back into the less than panoramic plot,
And opens the yellow book once more, and takes the blue
    man by the hand.

What one must have, will have, to prime the cause, at any
    cost,
Is the sense of the sensation, caught and always on its
    way—
Here in the book it cannot stay forever and there on the
    sea the text is lost.

The Choker

This is not the time for décolletage—
The last eye has plunged into those billows,
Lost care and caution in the milky sea:
Every man in the room a pearl diver,
And every woman pulling on the line.
A predatory hope is in the air—
Lascivious feet caught in the giant clam shell,
The brought-up bends of amorous pressure.

The woman now is through with verticals—
Who ever found, explored, caves of the heart,
So satisfied to filch the Sultan's Eye?
What better reason then to use the spoils
To tie a noose around the roving sea?—
You have seen these women with their chokers:
They have a high, closed, centripetal look,
And bead the circumstance upon a string.

Two images remain with the restless—
The woman herself puts down the pearls at night,
And the sea rolls into the glimmering coves,
The strand of pearls, a raft in the moonlight:
Until dawn, the antinomian wash.
That lithe, that brown-skinned diver on the rocks—
Of course, the woman wishes luck, then warns
Of long flotillas bumping overhead.

Colophon of the Rover

After the party, wine without wisdom, the heat of women
    and men,
He felt like an admiral who had come home to an empty
    room from a life at sea,

[79]

And the sunburned hand, before it was all too late, picked
    up the golden pen.

The smell of perfume and of smoke, the fast receding
    wave—
What made that last beautiful woman, breathless but not
    too bright,
Search the seaman in his eyes as if to ask: Am I the one
    you'll save?

Those young men poured into their dark suits, suppliant,
    surreal—
Have they gone to the black, uncharted islands looking for
    the lost twin Apollo
And left in this large, vacant place some strange,
    ambiguous appeal?

The pen, now a little tarnished, the hand more pallid,
    stroke by stroke—
Too many women stand on the glowing stone of a lavish
    ring:
You undress the one with warted skin, to one most fair,
    extend a cloak.

Thus I have seen these admiral sort of men showing
    nothing but a tip
Of gold clipped in a pocket as if they mean to leave unsaid
Savage sacrifices in the islands, imprinted on the air, the
    tattoo, lip by lip.

Yet there are those who come into a room—I wonder, am
    I one?
The incredible departure: nothing left to do—an aura and a
    pen—
The sunburned hand must move as if it would encroach
    upon some spreading stillness in the sun.